KU-646-691

Marley & Me
Meet Marley

HarperCollins*Publishers*

Meet Marley.

Marley is a playful puppy

who loves to make new friends.

He loves to play new games.

Marley is always on the go.

When Marley was born,

he was the smallest puppy

in his litter.

But Jenny doesn't mind.

"I think this is the dog

for us," says Jenny.

John takes Marley home

for the first time.

"This is your house," he says.

Marley is excited

to have a family.

Marley loves his new home.

But sometimes,

he has trouble following the rules.

Marley runs on the beach

without his collar and lead.

"Marley, no!" says John.

Marley makes a big mess

in the garage.

"Marley, no!" says Jenny.

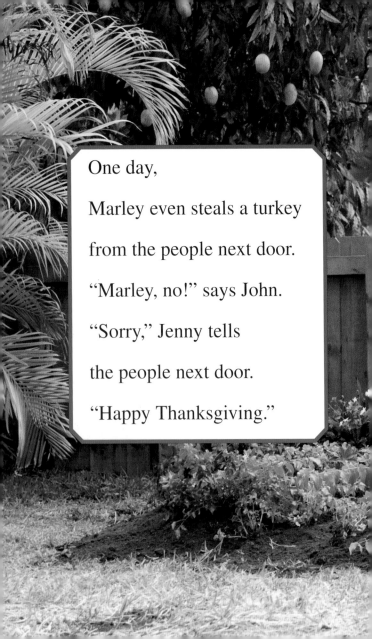

One day,

Marley even steals a turkey

from the people next door.

"Marley, no!" says John.

"Sorry," Jenny tells

the people next door.

"Happy Thanksgiving."

John and Jenny know

that Marley tries to be good.

They hope Marley will stop being wild

when he grows up.

But as Marley grows bigger,

he wants to eat more.

Marley starts chewing

nearly everything he sees.

Marley chews on the couch.

Marley chews the window blinds.

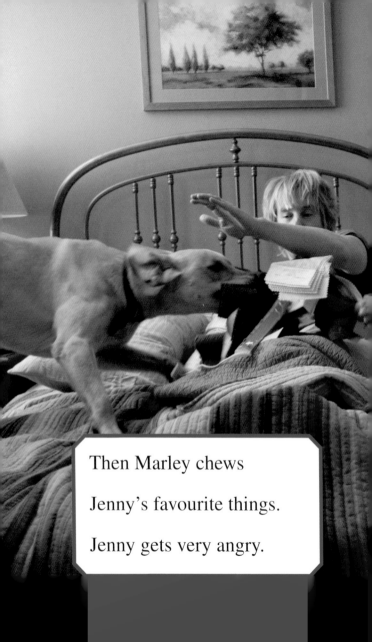

Then Marley chews

Jenny's favourite things.

Jenny gets very angry.

"Bad dog!" yells Jenny.

"Why do you do this?

Why do you wreck everything?"

Jenny is upset.

She asks John

to take Marley for a walk.

So John and Marley

go to the beach.

John does some thinking.

Marley does some thinking, too.

When Marley and John come home,

Jenny is happy to see them.

She feels much better.

"I'm sorry," Jenny tells Marley.

"I may get cross,

but we are still family."

Jenny and Marley start to dance.

Marley feels very happy.

The next day,

John, Jenny, and Marley

go to the beach to play.

"Good boy!" says John.

"Good boy!" says Jenny.

"We love you," they say.

Marley loves them, too.

Marley is a very lucky dog.

He has a family who loves him.

Who could ask for more?